PRESENTED TO

RECEIVED FROM

DATE

A 33-DAY JOURNEY OF
LOVE AND DEVOTION

INVITE HIM IN

and He Will
Take It From There.

Selah!

JAMES LOMAX *and*
VERNESTINE KENT LOMAX

INVITE HIM IN ... AND HE WILL TAKE IT FROM THERE. SELAH! A 33-Day Introspective Journey of Love and Devotion

© 2025 James and Vernestine Lomax

All rights reserved. No part of this publication may be reproduced, stored in a retrieval system, or transmitted in any form or by any means—electronic, mechanical, photocopying, recording, or otherwise—without the prior written permission of the authors, except for brief quotations used in reviews, articles, or other noncommercial uses permitted by copyright law. Published by and for permission requests, contact **The House of Lomax Publishing Company**
Email info@thehouseoflomax.com
All Scripture quotations, unless otherwise noted, are taken from the **King James Version (KJV)** of the Bible. Public Domain.

Cover by JBookDesigns and Interior iStock.com/©timonko iStock Order Number: 2103245486
Editor Anita Minniefield
Printed in the United States of America
ISBN (Paperback) 979-8-9992211-0-0
ISBN (eBook) 979-8-9992211-1-7
First Edition September 2025
Library of Congress Control Number: NCR114763

This devotional is a work of testimony and inspiration. Names, details, and events have been shared with integrity and prayer, reflecting the real-life story of the authors and God's divine orchestration. Portions of this work were developed with the assistance of ChatGPT, an AI language model created by OpenAI, under human authorship and prayerful editorial oversight.

DEDICATION

To **God**—our First Love, our Foundation, and our Matchmaker. Thank You for hearing the prayers we whispered and the ones we did not have the words to speak. Thank You for proving that when we surrender, You align every detail perfectly. This devotion is for Your glory.

To our **parents**—the late James and Mary Kent, James and Sallie Moore —your legacy of faith, love, and prayer created a covering we still feel today. Thank you for laying the spiritual groundwork that helped shape the people we have become.

To our **children**—Katherine, Hannah, and Jas—each of you is a testimony of God's grace. May you always know how deeply you are loved and how faithfully we continue to pray for God's perfect will in your lives.

To **Moses**, our son-in-love—thank you for loving Hannah as Christ loves the Church. We are grateful for your presence in our family.

To our precious **grandsons**, Malachi and Maverick—your joy reminds us daily of God's promises fulfilled across generations. May your lives be covered in prayer and purpose, just as ours have been.

And to **every single person** waiting on the Lord—whether you have never married, are healing from divorce, or walking through the valley of widowhood—this is for you. May this devotional rekindle your hope, refocus your faith, and remind you that God still writes love stories. Please know that your prayers are powerful. Your waiting is not wasted. Build with Him Trust Him. Invite Him in—and He will take it from there. Selah.

With all our love,
James & Vernestine

A WORD FROM US

When we look back over our Introspective Journey of Love and Devotion—individually and together—we see a tapestry only God could have woven. Our love story was not birthed in haste, nor by chance. It was birthed in prayer.

Before we ever met, there was an intercession. Before we said yes to each other, we said yes to God. This devotional and the life we now share stand as living proof that a foundation built on prayer is a foundation that stands.

You will notice throughout this devotional that the word "we" is used often. That "we" is us—James and Vernestine Lomax, a husband and wife brought together by divine timing, intercessory prayer, and God's undeniable hand.

This 33-day journey is not built on theory—it is built on testimony. Our love story was birthed in seasons of waiting, healing, surrender, and supernatural alignment. Every word you read flows from the unified voice of two hearts speaking as one. Hearts that were once navigating singleness and are now walking in covenant.

Prayer did not just prepare us for marriage—it aligned us with Heaven. It changed how we waited, how we healed, and how we walked in obedience. It was not a last resort. It was the first step. It was the blueprint. And it still is.

As you walk through these pages, know that we are not just sharing insights, we are sharing ourselves. Our prayer is that through our transparency, you will encounter God's faithfulness and find hope in unfolding your own story. He is building something sacred in your life, moment by moment, prayer by prayer. Just stay close with a bold expectation that God is writing your story with love, purpose, and grace.

~James & Vernestine

CONTENTS

DEDICATION v
FOREWORD xi
INTRODUCTION xv
ACKNOWLEDGMENTS xvii
HOW TO USE THIS DEVOTIONAL xix

Day 1	IT ALL BEGINS WITH PRAYER	1
Day 2	AGREEMENT UNLOCKS DESTINY	4
Day 3	TRUSTING IN GOD'S TIMING	7
Day 4	PREPARING YOUR HEART	10
Day 5	TRUSTING IN GOD'S PURPOSE	13
Day 6	SEEKING GOD ABOVE ALL ELSE	16
Day 7	SURRENDERING YOUR DESIRES TO GOD	19
Day 8	THE POWER OF PATIENCE	22
Day 9	STRENGTHENING YOUR FAITH	25
Day 10	BEAUTIFUL IN HIS TIME	28
Day 11	INTIMACY THROUGH PRAYER	31
Day 12	BUILDING YOUR INNER STRENGTH	34
Day 13	STRENGTH FOR THE SEASON YOU ARE IN	37
Day 14	ALIGNING YOUR DESIRES WITH GOD'S WILL . . .	40
Day 15	STRENGTH IN WAITING	43
Day 16	EMBRACING GOD'S TIMING	46
Day 17	PATIENCE IN PREPARATION	49
Day 18	TRUSTING IN GOD'S SOVEREIGNTY	52
Day 19	GUARDING YOUR HEART	55

Day 20	LEARNING TO BE CONTENT	58
Day 21	TRUSTING GOD'S PLAN	61
Day 22	PREPARING YOUR HEART FOR A RELATIONSHIP	64
Day 23	EMBRACING EMOTIONAL HEALING	67
Day 24	THE POWER OF FAITH IN WAITING	70
Day 25	EXPECTING GOD'S BEST	73
Day 26	PREPARING FOR MARRIAGE IN SPIRIT	76
Day 27	LIVING IN EXPECTATION	79
Day 28	TRUSTING THE PROCESS	82
Day 29	WALKING IN BOLDNESS	85
Day 30	BUILT BY THE LORD	88
Day 31	HEALING AFTER LOVE ENDS	91
Day 32	HONORING LOVE LOST, EMBRACING LOVE AHEAD	94
Day 33	COME: LET THE AUTHOR WRITE YOUR STORY	97

BLESSINGS & REFLECTIONS 101

FOREWORD

"Except the Lord build the house,
they labour in vain that build it.." (Psalm 127:1)

It is a sacred honor to write the foreword for this devotional, *Invite Him In… and He Will Take It From There. Selah!* I have walked alongside James and Vernestine as their spiritual covering, premarital counselor, and ultimately, the one blessed to pronounce them husband and wife. I have witnessed firsthand what happens when two people choose to build their love story on the unshakable foundation of prayer.

This devotional is not just pages of inspiration—it is a living testimony. It echoes the heartbeat of heaven: that when we surrender our timelines, open the doors of our hearts, and *invite Him in*, God begins to orchestrate a story greater than we could ever script. In this devotional, you will find truth and direction. This publication will help you endure and enjoy life and love in the manner God intended when He masterminded His divine plan for your life.

James and Vernestine's journey was not hurried, but holy. Their union was not born from chance, but from choice—God's choice. Before they ever laid eyes on each other, prayers were rising from multiple corners of the earth. Their niece, her husband, and Vernestine's sister stood in intercession for a full year. And God answered with divine clarity. This love story was birthed through fasting, through tears, through whispered hopes in the secret place. It is proof that when God writes the narrative, every chapter flows with purpose.

As you read each devotion entry, may you be reminded that God is still writing love stories. Whether you are single, divorced, or widowed, your heart is still known. Your story is still being shaped. Your prayers are not lost in the silence. He hears. He sees. And in His time, He answers.

Let this devotional stir your faith. Let it invite you into deeper intimacy with the One who knows the desires of your heart. And most importantly, let it inspire you to trust again, pray again, and believe again.

I bless this work, and I bless every reader who will journey through these 33 days of devotion. May it mark a turning point, a rekindling of hope, and a divine alignment with God's perfect plan. Remember that the people who know their God shall be strong and do exploits.

With Apostolic Love and Covering,

++Archbishop Lorenzo N. Peterson, ThD
Metropolitan Archbishop, International Alliance Communion, McDonough, Georgia
Officiant of the Holy Union of James & Vernestine Lomax

FOREWORD

Reverend James and Elder Vernestine Lomax have truly heard from heaven. Their willingness to wait on God and pursue Him through prayer has produced what I can only describe as a divine union—one I have had the privilege to witness firsthand.

This devotional and collection of reflections is the outpouring of two lives shaped individually by communion with God. Every page carries the weight of intercession, hope, love, and faithful obedience. These devotions will allow you to experience and encounter the presence of God in a fresh, new way.

I've walked alongside Reverend Lomax not only as a friend but also as a fellow servant in ministry. His prophetic voice, steady leadership, and unwavering commitment to Christ have remained constant over the 30+ years I've known him. By his side stands Elder Vernestine, his true rib—a woman of profound faith and fervent prayer, marked by an unshakable desire to please God in all she does.

This 33-day introspective journey of love and devotion sets God's order and will align you with His perfect will instead of His permissive will. I've heard our Pastor, Bishop Dale C. Bronner, say, "If you think it, ink it." There is power in journaling, and this masterpiece from heaven allows you to engage with God in a new and fresh way daily while preparing your heart to receive God's best for you and your future spouse.

My prayer is that as you journey through these pages, you will be drawn closer to the heart of the Father, and that the example of James and Vernestine Lomax will inspire you to wait on the Lord and be of good courage. And while you are waiting, God is preparing your spouse even as you read these words. With honor,

Reverend Bryan Allen
Congregational and Online Care Pastor
Word of Faith Family Worship Cathedral
Mableton, Georgia

INTRODUCTION

Before we ever saw each other, we prayed. Before we ever loved each other, we listened for God's voice. This devotional, *Invite Him In ... and He Will Take It From There. Selah!*, is not just our story, it is an invitation. An invitation to trust that God is not only aware of your desire for a godly mate, but that He is already at work—laying the groundwork, moving in the unseen, and preparing hearts on both sides.

Our journey began long before our first conversation. For an entire year, unseen hands lifted prayers for our union. Loved ones prayed day after day, without knowing the names or faces of the people they were interceding for. And yet, God heard. He saw. And in His perfect timing, He moved.

When we finally did meet—438 miles apart—what should have felt like a coincidence was undeniably God. James had seen me in a vision during prayer. I had been praying over a list for my future husband. We both had surrendered our desires at the altar, trusting that if the foundation were built on prayer, then what stood upon it would never crumble.

This devotional is about not rushing ahead, not settling out of weariness, but building from the ground up, with God at the center.

If you are single, divorced, or widowed and believing God for a mate, we wrote this for you. Every entry reflects how prayer carried us, connected us, and confirmed what only heaven could orchestrate.

Let this 33-day Introspective Journey guide your heart back to the One who sees all and knows all. May each scripture, reflection, prayer, and action step draw you closer to the God who still writes love stories, and may your story be built, like ours, on the unshakable foundation of prayer.

ACKNOWLEDGMENTS

First and foremost, we acknowledge *our Lord and Savior Jesus Christ,* the Author and Finisher of our faith. Thank You, Father, for every divine detail, every whispered promise, and every answered prayer. This devotional is a reflection of Your faithfulness in our lives.

To the *three intercessors* who prayed faithfully for 365 days—*Laverne, Anthony, and Teresa*—your obedience to the Spirit opened the heavens over our lives. Thank you for standing in the gap, for believing in a promise you could not yet see. You taught us what it means to labor in love and to wait with expectancy.

To our *spiritual mentors, pastors, and prayer warriors* who covered us individually and as a couple, your wisdom and words were the bricks that helped build our foundation.

To our *family and friends,* thank you for walking with us, encouraging us, and celebrating the unfolding of God's plan. Your love and support mean more than words can say.

To every *single person reading this devotional,* your journey matters. Your prayers are heard. Your faith is not in vain. We see you. We honor your hope. And we stand with you in belief that God will do what He promised.

Finally, to one another—James and Vernestine—thank you for saying yes to God first, so we could say yes to each other. This book is only possible because we chose to INVITE HIM IN to build it all—*together*—on a foundation built on prayer ... AND HE TOOK IT FROM THERE. SELAH.

HOW TO USE THIS DEVOTIONAL

This devotional, *Invite Him In ... and He Will Take It From There. Selah!* is more than just daily reading; it is an invitation into a sacred, personal journey with God as you prepare for the love He has promised. Whether you are never-married, divorced, or widowed, this journey is designed to stir your faith, ignite your hope, and anchor your heart in the truth that God is faithful to fulfill every promise, especially when it comes to love.

Each of the 33 daily entries includes

- A Scripture to meditate on
- A short devotion drawn from our real-life love story, grounded in prayer
- A prayer to lift your heart to God
- An action step to activate your faith, and
- A meditation prompt to reflect and hear from the Holy Spirit

Here's how to walk through this journey

1. Set Sacred Time
Choose a quiet space and dedicate intentional time each day to meet with God. Mornings are powerful, but anytime your heart is open is the right time. Bring a journal, an open Bible, and your full attention.

2. Read with Expectancy
Approach each entry believing God will speak directly to you. This journey is not about rushing; it is about realignment, revelation, and renewal. Let every word encourage you, challenge you, and deepen your desire for Him.

3. Pray the Prayers Aloud

There is power in speaking life over your situation. Declare the prayers over yourself daily. Add your own words as you feel led. Do not be afraid to repeat them throughout the day; faith comes by hearing.

4. Act on Your Faith

Each action step is simple, but intentional. These are not chores; they are sacred opportunities to mate with God. The steps are designed to help you become the person who is ready to receive the love you are praying for.

5. Reflect and Listen

The meditations will help you pause, reflect, and write what God is showing you. These are holy moments. The word Selah – found throughout the devotional – means to pause and calmly reflect. Let this be your posture as you record your insights, your emotions, and your prayers answered. These written moments will become a personal record of how God met you in the waiting.

6. Revisit and Repeat

God's Word is alive. You may feel led to return to a particular devotion entry multiple times. That is okay. This is your personal journey, go at God's pace.

Remember this: You are not just preparing for a relationship, you are preparing for a purpose-filled union that glorifies God. And that begins with a foundation built on prayer. Invite Him in, and He will take it from there. Selah

DAY 1

IT ALL BEGINS WITH PRAYER

SCRIPTURE

"Again I say unto you, That if two of you shall agree on earth as touching anything that they shall ask, it shall be done for them of my Father which is in heaven."
(Matthew 18:19)

JOURNEY OF LOVE AND DEVOTION

Before we ever laid eyes on each other, a foundation was already being built through prayer. What's amazing is that a small group of people had committed to interceding for our relationship for an entire year, even though we had never met. Their prayers created space for God to move and reveal His will.

While James was in Georgia, praying for the wife God had for him, I (Vernestine) was in North Carolina with my own prayer list for a husband. Neither of us knew what God was doing behind the scenes, but we were both preparing through prayer.

You might be in that same season right now, waiting, wondering, hoping. But here's the truth, your prayers are laying the groundwork. Each one you whisper is part of something bigger. You are not just waiting, you are mating with God to build your future on the firmest foundation there is Him.

So do not stop praying. Do not lose heart. Invite God into the deepest parts of your desire. Let prayer be the blueprint for what's to come.

A PRAYER FOR YOU

Heavenly Father, I come to You with a heart open to Your will. You see every desire, every prayer I have prayed in private. Help me to trust that You are working even when I cannot see it. Teach me to prepare, to pray with purpose, and to believe that my future is being shaped in the secret place. In Jesus' name, Amen.

AN INTROSPECTIVE ACTION

Start a quiet moment today by opening a fresh page in your journal and titling it *"Prayers for My Future Spouse."* Write down your heart's desires: specific character traits, values you want to share, and the spiritual foundation you are praying to build together. Do not hold back, be honest, be intentional, and trust that God is attentive to every detail you place before Him. Let this become your altar of hope.

A MEDITATIVE THOUGHT

Reflect on Matthew 18:19. Envision God leaning in, attentive, present, as you speak your prayers aloud. Let the weight of His promise anchor you, *"If two of you shall agree..."* It is not just words, it is a covenant. Trust that every prayer you lift in alignment with His will is already at work, shaping what your eyes cannot yet behold. Believe that the foundation you are building in prayer is securing something eternal, Selah!

UP CLOSE & PERSONAL

It All Begins with Prayer. When you invite Him in, you create space for divine alignment, healing, and hope. Whether you are navigating life as someone who's never been married, walking through healing after a divorce, or carrying the sacred memories of a spouse who has passed, this devotion speaks to your season. Your story matters to God, and He is not finished with your love story.

> *"Prayer is not preparation for the promise*
> *—it is the foundation on which it stands."*

JOURNAL YOUR THOUGHTS

_____

_____

_____

_____

_____

_____

_____

DAY 2
AGREEMENT UNLOCKS DESTINY

SCRIPTURE

"Can two walk together, except they be agreed?"
(Amos 3:3)

JOURNEY OF LOVE AND DEVOTION

One of the most beautiful parts of our story is how alignment in prayer brought divine agreement. Even before we met, our prayers were in harmony, though we did not know it at the time. We both desired to walk with someone who was fully surrendered to God. That agreement in spirit laid the path to destiny.

It was not just our prayers; her niece, her husband, who is my best friend, and my wife's sister were praying, too. We did not collaborate, yet our hearts were synchronized. There is a spiritual power in agreement. When our prayers align with God's heart, and when others intercede with us in unity, it invites Heaven to respond.

You may feel like you are praying alone right now, but you are not. God hears, and He responds to agreement. Seek people of faith who can agree with you in prayer. Ask God to align your heart with the one He is preparing for you. Agreement unlocks destiny.

A PRAYER FOR YOU

Heavenly Father, I want to walk in agreement with Your perfect will. If I have been praying from a place of fear, disappointment, or frustration, realign my heart with faith and trust. Help me to find people who will agree with me in prayer, people who believe in Your timing and Your plans. I pray that my future mate and I will be united in spirit, even before we meet. In Jesus' name, Amen.

AN INTROSPECTIVE ACTION

Take a bold step of faith today—reach out to one trusted friend or family member and invite them to stand in agreement with you in prayer. Share one heartfelt desire you are lifting before God about your future relationship. Then, commit to praying together once a week this month. There is power in agreement. Let your prayers unite and strengthen the foundation you are building for what is to come.

A MEDITATIVE THOUGHT

Breathe deeply and sit with Amos 3:3, *"Can two walk together, except they be agreed?"* In the stillness, ask yourself—*Am I walking in step with God's will for my life and future relationship?* Invite the Holy Spirit to gently uncover any areas misaligned with His purpose. As He reveals, write them down, not in shame, but in surrender. Let this be a moment of realignment, where your desires and His design come into agreement.

UP CLOSE & PERSONAL

Agreement Unlocks Destiny. No matter if you have never stood at the altar, once said 'I do' and now walk alone, or cherish the love of one who's gone home to glory, this devotion meets you where you are. Your season is seen by God. Your story is not over. God knows the combination to unlock your destiny. He is still unlocking and writing your love story, with purpose, with hope, and with divine timing.

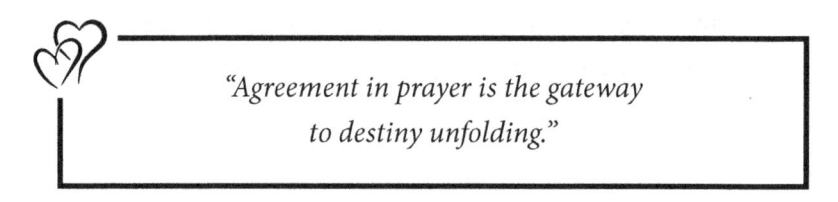

> *"Agreement in prayer is the gateway to destiny unfolding."*

JOURNAL YOUR THOUGHTS

_____
_____
_____
_____
_____
_____
_____
_____
_____
_____
_____

DAY 3
TRUSTING IN GOD'S TIMING

SCRIPTURE

"To everything there is a season, and a time to every purpose under the heaven"
(Ecclesiastes 3:1)

JOURNEY OF LOVE AND DEVOTION

When we reflect on our journey, one thing is clear: God's timing was everything. We did not rush it. We did not try to force things to happen. Instead, we patiently trusted that God would bring us together at the right moment.

During that year of prayer, when we did not even know each other existed, our family was praying with unwavering faith. Little did they know, God was aligning us for our future, step by step. Had we met earlier, we may not have been ready. But in God's perfect timing, everything fell into place.

As you wait for God's best, remember He is never in a hurry. His timing is flawless, and His purpose is always bigger than we can imagine.

Trust that every prayer you lift up is being heard, and that God is preparing you and your future spouse for something beautiful. The waiting is not wasted, it is part of the process.

A PRAYER FOR YOU

Heavenly Father, I confess that I sometimes get impatient, and I wonder if I will ever meet the right person. But I trust Your perfect timing. Help me to wait with grace and to continue seeking You in this season of preparation. Teach me to trust that You are working behind the scenes, even when I cannot see the full picture. I believe when the time is right, You will bring us together. In Jesus' name, Amen.

AN INTROSPECTIVE ACTION

Identify one area in your life where trusting God's timing feels especially hard. Sit with it, name it honestly. Then, release it to Him in prayer, surrendering the weight you have been carrying. Write your thoughts in a journal, not to fix it, but to free it. Ask God to exchange your anxiety for His peace as you wait, knowing His timing is never late and always purposeful.

A MEDITATIVE THOUGHT

Reflect and let Ecclesiastes 3:1 wash over you, *"To everything there is a season, and a time to every purpose under the heaven."* Reflect on the seasons you have walked through: the joys, the delays, the lessons wrapped in waiting. Each one had a purpose. Now, invite God to still your heart in this present season. Whisper this truth to your spirit: His timing is perfect, and what is meant for you will arrive right on time. Rest here. Trust here. Wait here—with peace.

UP CLOSE & PERSONAL

Trusting God's Timing. If you are single by choice, circumstance, or sacred memory, this devotion meets you in your season. Your story still matters to God. He hasn't forgotten you, and He's not late. Trust that His timing is perfect, and your love story is unfolding exactly as He designed for you and your mate.

> *"God's timing is not a delay; it's a divine design for your good"*

JOURNAL YOUR THOUGHTS

_____
_____
_____
_____
_____
_____
_____
_____
_____
_____

DAY 4

PREPARING YOUR HEART

SCRIPTURE

"Create in me a clean heart, O God; and renew a right spirit within me."
(Psalm 51:10)

JOURNEY OF LOVE AND DEVOTION

Before we could meet, God had to prepare our hearts. The journey was not just about finding each other; it was about being ready to receive each other. It was not just about love; it was about emotional and spiritual maturity.

During that year of prayer, our hearts had to be aligned with God's will. There were things we needed to heal from, things we needed to release, and qualities we needed to develop. We were not yet the people we needed to be for one another. But as we prayed and trusted in God's timing, He worked in us, preparing us for the life we would one day share.

Your preparation is not just about finding the right person, it is about becoming the right person. Ask God to search your heart, reveal areas that need healing, and help you grow in the areas that will make you a better mate.

A PRAYER FOR YOU

Heavenly Father, I invite You to examine my heart. Show me the areas where I need healing or growth. Help me to prepare my heart and spirit for the one You are preparing for me. I trust that as I grow, You are preparing them too. May I always seek Your will first, trusting that You will bring us together at the perfect time, and that we will be ready for one another. In Jesus' name, Amen.

AN INTROSPECTIVE ACTION

Take a moment to reflect on areas in your life where you need healing, growth, or emotional maturity. Ask God to work in those areas and bring you closer to the person He wants you to become. Write down your thoughts and pray through them.

A MEDITATIVE THOUGHT

Think about Psalm 51:10, *"Create in me a clean heart, O God; and renew a right spirit within me."* Ask God to give you a pure heart, one that is ready for the relationship He has in store for you. Meditate on the areas where God is leading you to grow. Trust that as you prepare, He is also preparing your future mate.

UP CLOSE & PERSONAL

Preparing Your Heart. If your love has not come, came and left, or left you with a trust of memories, this devotion meets you in your season. God knows the condition of your heart, and your story still matters to God. He has not forgotten you, and He's not late. This is a heart matter, and He is carefully crafting the perfect love story for your life.

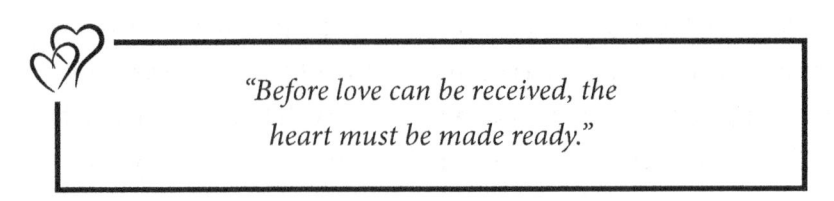

> *"Before love can be received, the heart must be made ready."*

JOURNAL YOUR THOUGHTS

DAY 5
TRUSTING IN GOD'S PURPOSE

SCRIPTURE

"For I know the thoughts that I think toward you, saith the Lord, thoughts of peace, and not of evil, to give you an expected end."
(Jeremiah 29:11)

JOURNEY OF LOVE AND DEVOTION

One of the most powerful revelations we had during that year of prayer was that God's purpose for our lives was always greater than our own desires. At the time, we had no idea what was coming. But we trusted that God had a plan, and we surrendered to it, knowing He was orchestrating everything behind the scenes.

As we prayed, we each had our own expectations of what we wanted in a spouse. But as we grew in prayer, God began to reveal His greater purpose for our lives. We began to realize that we were not just praying for a companion, we were praying for someone to walk with us in the mission God had for us. Our union was not just for our happiness, but for His glory.

Trusting in God's purpose means surrendering your own plans. It means believing that the life He has for you, with the person He's preparing for you, will be far greater than you could ever imagine.

A PRAYER FOR YOU

Heavenly Father, I surrender my desires, my timeline, and my plans to You. I trust Your purpose for my life. Help me to believe that You know what is best for me, even when I cannot see it yet. Align my heart with Your will and give me the patience to wait for Your perfect plan to unfold. In Jesus' name, Amen.

AN INTROSPECTIVE ACTION

Set aside a quiet moment today to reflect honestly on your heart's desires for a relationship. Write down any expectations, longings, or fears that rise to the surface. Do not filter, just be real. Then, lift each one to God in prayer, surrendering them with open hands. Ask Him to reveal His truth to you. Trust that even now, He is faithfully working behind the scenes on your behalf.

A MEDITATIVE THOUGHT

Selah. Rest in the promise of Jeremiah 29:11, *"For I know the thoughts that I think toward you,"* declares the Heavenly Father, *"thoughts of peace, and not of evil, to give you an expected end."* Let these words settle deep in your spirit. Reflect on the ways God has already shown Himself faithful; how He's guided, protected, and provided. Now, release every worry about what's ahead. You do not have to figure it all out. He already has. Breathe in His peace, and breathe out your fears. He's not just planning your future—He's holding it.

UP CLOSE & PERSONAL

Trusting in God's Purpose. It does not matter if you are still waiting on love, healing from love lost, or honoring love that lives on in your heart, this devotion meets you in your season. Your story still matters to God. Don't give up. Trust in His purpose. He knows just what you need. He hasn't forgotten you, and He's not late. Trust that His purpose is perfect, and your love story is unfolding exactly as He designed.

> *"When you surrender your plans, you make room for God's purpose."*

JOURNAL YOUR THOUGHTS

DAY 6
SEEKING GOD ABOVE ALL ELSE

SCRIPTURE

"But seek ye first the kingdom of God, and his righteousness; and all these things shall be added unto you."
(Matthew 6:33)

JOURNEY OF LOVE AND DEVOTION

When we look back at the beginning of our relationship, one thing stands out: we both sought God above everything else. We did not rush into a relationship because we were lonely or looking for fulfillment. We each made it our priority to seek God's will first and foremost.

There were times when we prayed fervently, asking God to guide us toward the right person. But it was not until we truly sought His kingdom and righteousness that everything else began to fall into place. Our focus shifted from seeking a spouse to seeking God. That is when He aligned our desires with His plan.

Seeking God above all else is about shifting your perspective. It is about letting go of the pressure to find the "right" person and focusing on becoming the right person, through God's grace. Trust that as you make God the priority, He will lead you in the direction of your divine mate.

A PRAYER FOR YOU

Heavenly Father, I choose to seek You above all else today. I surrender my desire for a spouse and place it in Your hands. Help me to prioritize You above my own plans and expectations. May my heart be fully aligned with Yours, trusting that as I seek You, You will guide me to the person You have prepared for me. In Jesus' name, Amen.

AN INTROSPECTIVE ACTION

Take time today to reflect on the things you are prioritizing in your life. Ask yourself if God is truly first in your heart. If not, make a conscious decision to redirect your focus. Spend intentional time seeking God through prayer, scripture, or worship, and invite Him to align your heart with His.

A MEDITATIVE THOUGHT

Reflect on Matthew 6:33, *"But seek ye first the kingdom of God, and his righteousness; and all these things shall be added unto you."* Take a moment to pray and seek God's kingdom first, not just for your relationship but in all areas of your life. Trust that as you place Him at the center, He will add the right things in His perfect timing.

UP CLOSE & PERSONAL

Seeking God Above All Else. No matter your season—whether you've never been married, are walking through the healing journey after a divorce, or carrying the honor of a spouse who has passed—this devotion calls you to fix your eyes on God first. Your love story is not on hold; it is being written by the Author of your soul. He sees your heart, and He knows your desires. In His perfect time and way, everything else—including the desires of your heart—will be added. He is not withholding. He is aligning. Keep your eyes on the One who holds your story in His hands.

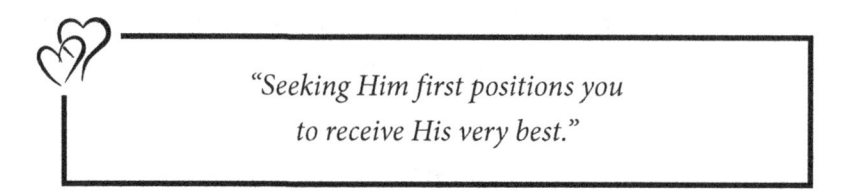

> *"Seeking Him first positions you to receive His very best."*

JOURNAL YOUR THOUGHTS

_____

_____

_____

_____

_____

_____

_____

_____

DAY 7

SURRENDERING YOUR DESIRES TO GOD

SCRIPTURE

"Trust in the Lord with all thine heart; and lean not unto thine own understanding. In all thy ways acknowledge him, and he shall direct thy paths."
(Proverbs 3:5-6)

JOURNEY OF LOVE AND DEVOTION

One of the most important lessons we learned during our time of prayer before meeting each other was the art of surrender. We had our own desires and expectations of what we thought our futures would look like, especially when it came to relationships. But as we spent more time in prayer, we began to realize that God's plans were so much better.

In the beginning, we held onto our ideal picture of a spouse and how we thought things should unfold. But God gently reminded us that His understanding of what we needed was far more accurate than our own. Just like how we were each praying independently and unknowingly for one another, God knew exactly when we were both ready to meet. It was in surrendering our desires, dreams, and expectations that God showed us His plan was perfect, and perfectly timed.

When we surrender our desires to God, we make space for Him to move. Our hearts become aligned with His, and we open the door for His direction. This kind of surrender is not about giving up; it is about giving in to what He has in store for us.

A PRAYER FOR YOU

Heavenly Father, I surrender my desires for a relationship to You. I trust that You know what is best for me, and Your plans are better than mine. Help me to let go of any expectations or anxieties I have about the future and trust You. As I acknowledge You today, I know You will direct my path. In Jesus' name, Amen.

AN INTROSPECTIVE ACTION

Spend some time today reflecting on areas in your life where you might be holding onto your own desires too tightly. Write down any expectations you have for your future spouse and relationship. Now, take a moment to release these expectations to God, surrendering them and trusting Him to guide you.

A MEDITATIVE THOUGHT

Reflect on Proverbs 3:5-6, *"Trust in the Lord with all thine heart; and lean not unto thine own understanding. In all thy ways acknowledge him, and he shall direct thy paths."* Meditate on the idea of trusting God with your heart's desires for a spouse. Take a deep breath and allow the peace of surrender to fill you, knowing that God is in control of your path.

UP CLOSE & PERSONAL

Surrendering Your Desires to God. Your path may be untouched by vows, marked by pain, or graced by eternity's embrace. This devotion meets you in your season. The key to your future is surrender. Your story still matters to God. He hasn't forgotten you, and He's not late. Keep surrendering your desires to him as He continues to unfold your love story.

> *"Surrendering is not giving up;
> it's giving God the reins."*

JOURNAL YOUR THOUGHTS

DAY 8
THE POWER OF PATIENCE

SCRIPTURE

"Wait on the Lord be of good courage, and he shall strengthen thine heart: wait, I say, on the Lord."
(Psalm 27:14)

JOURNEY OF LOVE AND DEVOTION

Patience is one of the most significant aspects of our journey. We both had to learn to wait; wait for God's timing, wait for His preparation, and wait for the right moment when we would come together. The process was not always easy. It required trust and courage to hold onto faith, even when it seemed like nothing was happening.

The year of prayer was not just about asking God for a spouse, it was about trusting that He was working behind the scenes. We did not know each other yet, but God knew exactly when we were both ready to meet. And He made sure that we were both prepared to step into the relationship He had designed for us.

Patience is not passive. It is an *active* waiting, a trust-filled waiting. It is knowing that while we wait, God is strengthening us, preparing us, and making us ready for the person He has chosen for us. It is about believing that God's timing is perfect, even when it feels like you are in a season of waiting.

A PRAYER FOR YOU

Heavenly Father, help me to trust in Your timing. Give me the strength to wait with patience, knowing that You are at work. Strengthen my heart, Heavenly Father, and help me to be of good courage as I wait for Your perfect timing. In Jesus' name, Amen.

AN INTROSPECTIVE ACTION

Take a moment today to reflect on the areas where you may struggle with patience. Are there areas in your life where you are trying to rush ahead or take control? Surrender these to God, ask Him to give you the strength to wait on His timing. Write down any feelings of impatience you have and ask God to help you trust in His process.

A MEDITATIVE THOUGHT

Reflect on Psalm 27:14, *"Wait on the Lord be of good courage, and he shall strengthen thine heart: wait, I say, on the Lord."* Allow the peace of waiting on the Lord to fill your heart. Let go of any anxieties about the future and focus on the promise that God is strengthening you as you wait. Trust that His timing is always perfect, and His plan for you will unfold in due season.

UP CLOSE & PERSONAL

The Power of Patience. You could be discovering what love means, recovering from where it hurt, or reflecting on what once was. This devotion meets you in the waiting. God sees where you are, and He's not late. Let patience have its perfect way. While you are discovering, recovering, or reflecting, know this: His delays are never denials, they are divine preparations. Your story is still unfolding, and the Author is faithful. Trust that your waiting is not wasted. In His perfect time, God will reveal His Masterpiece.

> *"Patience is the bridge between your prayer and God's promise."*

JOURNAL YOUR THOUGHTS

_____
_____
_____
_____
_____
_____
_____
_____
_____

DAY 9
STRENGTHENING YOUR FAITH

SCRIPTURE

"So then faith cometh by hearing, and hearing by the word of God."
(Romans 10:17)

JOURNEY OF LOVE AND DEVOTION

In the waiting season, faith can be tested in unexpected ways. As we spent our time praying and waiting for the person God had for us, our faith was often challenged. There were moments when doubt crept in, and we wondered if God had forgotten about us or if our prayers were being heard. But what we came to realize is that the waiting period was not a time of inactivity, it was a time of growth.

During this season, we made it a priority to immerse ourselves in God's Word. The more time we spent reading Scripture, the more our faith was built up. Faith comes by hearing, and hearing by the Word of God. It was through daily doses of truth from the Bible that we found the strength to keep going. We learned that God's promises are sure, and His timing is perfect.

Faith in the waiting is not about pretending everything is okay; it is about believing in God's goodness and His faithfulness, even when we cannot see the whole picture. Just as we were praying and seeking God independently, He was building our faith to prepare us for the future He had planned for us.

A PRAYER FOR YOU

Heavenly Father, during this season of waiting, I choose to strengthen my faith in You. Help me to trust that You are working even when I cannot see it. Teach me to rely on Your Word to strengthen my spirit. I know that my faith will grow as I focus on You and Your promises. Help me to rest in Your faithfulness and trust that You are preparing me for the future You have in store. In Jesus' name, Amen.

AN INTROSPECTIVE ACTION

Today, set aside time to read and reflect on a Scripture that strengthens your faith. It could be one that has spoken to you before or one that the Holy Spirit leads you to. As you read, let it sink deep into your heart. Write down any thoughts or feelings that come up and pray over them, trusting God to strengthen your faith in the waiting.

A MEDITATIVE THOUGHT

Reflect on Romans 10:17, "So then faith cometh by hearing, and hearing by the word of God." Meditate on how the Word of God builds your faith. As you wait, let Scripture remind you of God's goodness, His promises, and His faithfulness. Trust that your faith is being strengthened in this season, even if it does not feel like much is happening.

UP CLOSE & PERSONAL

Strengthening Your Faith. Whether you have never been married, are healing from the wounds of divorce, or carry the sacred memory of a love once shared, know this: your season of waiting is not empty, it is sacred. Faith is strengthened when you choose to believe before you see, when you cling to the Word in the silence, and when you trust that God's promises still stand. Let His Word be your daily bread, and trust that every unseen moment is working to prepare something eternal. Your faith isn't fragile, it's being fortified..

> *"Faith grows not in answers, but in the waiting."*

JOURNAL YOUR THOUGHTS

_____

_____

_____

_____

_____

_____

_____

DAY 10
BEAUTIFUL IN HIS TIME

SCRIPTURE

"He hath made everything beautiful in his time: also he hath set the world in their heart, so that no man can find out the work that God maketh from the beginning to the end."
(Ecclesiastes 3:11)

JOURNEY OF LOVE AND DEVOTION

Trusting God's timing is one of the most defining lessons we have learned on our journey to finding each other. It was easy to want to rush things, to look around and see others in relationships, and wonder when our time would come. But over time, we realized that God's timing is not just about when things happen, it is about the beauty He creates in the waiting.

When we reflect on the year of prayer before we met, we see how God's timing was at work in every detail. There was no rush, no pressure, just a steady unfolding of His plan. The beauty of God's timing is that it is perfect and purposeful. He knows exactly when we are ready, when our hearts are aligned, and when we are fully prepared for the person He has for us.

God is never in a hurry, and He is never late. His timing is intentional, and when we trust Him, we can rest in the assurance that everything will come together at just the right moment. Just as we were both being prepared in our individual walks with God, His timing brought us together at the perfect time.

A PRAYER FOR YOU

Heavenly Father, I confess that at times I have struggled with trusting Your timing. Help me to understand that You make everything beautiful in Your time. Teach me to trust that You are at work in my life, even when I cannot see the full picture. Give me peace as I wait for Your best for me. In Jesus' name, Amen.

AN INTROSPECTIVE ACTION

Reflect on any areas where you may struggle to trust God's timing. Are there moments when you feel anxious about the future? Write down these feelings and give them to God. Ask Him to help you trust that He is in control and that His timing will bring about what is best for you.

A MEDITATIVE THOUGHT

Reflect on Ecclesiastes 3:11, *"He hath made everything beautiful in his time: also he hath set the world in their heart, so that no man can find out the work that God maketh from the beginning to the end."* Meditate on the idea that everything is beautiful in God's time. Trust that, even if you cannot see the bigger picture, God's plan for your life is unfolding at the perfect pace. Rest in knowing that He is working all things together for your good.

UP CLOSE & PERSONAL

Beautiful In His Time. Your heart might be seeking connection, mending from separation, or cherishing a sacred moment; this devotion understands where you are in your season. Your story still matters to God, and it is beautiful. He hasn't forgotten you, and He's not late. Trust that His process is perfect, and your love story will be beautiful in His time.

> *"God's process is not just time, but transformation."*

JOURNAL YOUR THOUGHTS

DAY 11
INTIMACY THROUGH PRAYER

SCRIPTURE

"Pray without ceasing."
(1 Thessalonians 5:17)

JOURNEY OF LOVE AND DEVOTION

We were constantly in prayer during our journey. Prayer became our communication with God, and we learned how essential it is to speak with Him daily. For singles, prayer is not just about asking for a spouse—it is about building a relationship with God. It is about continually seeking Him, learning His voice, and trusting in His will for your life.

As we prayed together, we found that the more we communicated with God, the more we felt His presence guiding us. Prayer has become our source of strength, clarity, and peace. It was in prayer that we were reminded of God's faithfulness and His perfect plan for our lives.

For you, prayer is your lifeline. Use it to draw closer to God, build intimacy with Him, and trust that He is working on your behalf. Please know that God is preparing you and your future spouse in ways you cannot yet see.

A PRAYER FOR YOU

Heavenly Father, teach me the power of prayer in building my relationship with You. I want to constantly pray, seeking Your will and trusting in Your guidance. Help me to pray not only for my future spouse but for the wisdom and peace I need each day. In Jesus' name, Amen.

AN INTROSPECTIVE ACTION

Commit to a daily prayer time, whether short or long. Set aside a few minutes each day to speak with God, seeking His will for your life and future relationship. Write down any insights or desires during your time in prayer.

A MEDITATIVE THOUGHT

Reflect on 1 Thessalonians 5:17 and *"praying without ceasing."* See prayer as a continuous conversation with God, where you seek guidance and strengthen your relationship with Him. Embrace prayer as your most valuable tool in this season.

UP CLOSE & PERSONAL

Intimacy Through Prayer. Your story of love may still be unfolding, may have left you with lessons, or may live on as a legacy. This devotion invites you deeper into God's presence. Your story still matters to Him. He hears every whispered prayer and sees the longings of your heart. Prayer is not just preparation for love; it is where intimacy with God is formed. As you seek Him, trust He is drawing near, responding in love, and writing a story rooted in divine connection. Let your prayer life be where healing begins and new love is nurtured.

> *"Prayer is not just the path to your promise; it is the place where you fall in love with God first."*

JOURNAL YOUR THOUGHTS

DAY 12

BUILDING YOUR INNER STRENGTH

SCRIPTURE

"But they that wait upon the Lord shall renew their strength; they shall mount up with wings as eagles; they shall run, and not be weary; and they shall walk, and not faint."
(Isaiah 40:31)

JOURNEY OF LOVE AND DEVOTION

In the waiting season, it is easy to feel weak, frustrated, or discouraged. However, this is the perfect time to allow God to strengthen us from the inside out. As we waited, God was working in our hearts, refining us and making us more resilient.

We faced many moments of uncertainty during our wait, but each challenge strengthened our faith. We learned to lean into God's strength, especially during moments of doubt. It was through the power of God's Word and His promises that we found the courage to press on.

For you, building inner strength means trusting God to renew your spirit. It means allowing Him to fill you with peace, joy, and a sense of purpose. Take this season as an opportunity to grow in strength, knowing that God is preparing you for something beautiful.

A PRAYER FOR YOU

Heavenly Father, I ask that You renew my strength as I wait on You. Help me to rely on Your power rather than my own. Fill me with peace, joy, and strength so that I may continue to trust in Your perfect plan for my life. In Jesus' name, Amen.

AN INTROSPECTIVE ACTION

Identify and write down one area where you feel weak or discouraged in your waiting season. Pray over this area, asking God to renew your strength and fill you with courage.

A MEDITATIVE THOUGHT

Reflect on Isaiah 40:31, *"But they that wait upon the Lord shall renew their strength; they shall mount up with wings as eagles; they shall run, and not be weary; and they shall walk, and not faint,"* and allow it to renew your spirit. Trust that God is strengthening you even in the waiting. Take comfort in knowing that as you wait on the Heavenly Father, He will give you the inner strength you need to endure and grow.

UP CLOSE & PERSONAL

Building Your Inner Strength. Perhaps you are still waiting for love, weeping through a parting, or whispering goodbye to someone you will always hold dear. This devotion reminds you that strength is being built in the waiting. God sees every moment you've endured, and He is using this season to fortify your faith, renew your spirit, and anchor your hope. Your story still matters to Him. You are not forgotten, and you are not weak; you are being strengthened for what's ahead. Trust that as you wait, He prepares you to rise with renewed strength, ready for the love He's still writing into your life.

> *"Waiting on God renews strength that the world cannot offer."*

JOURNAL YOUR THOUGHTS

_____

_____

_____

_____

_____

_____

_____

_____

_____

_____

_____

_____

DAY 13

STRENGTH FOR THE SEASON YOU ARE IN

SCRIPTURE

"Be patient therefore, brethren, unto the coming of the Lord. Behold, the husbandman waiteth for the precious fruit of the earth, and hath long patience for it, until he receives the early and latter rain."
(James 5:7)

JOURNEY OF LOVE AND DEVOTION

Patience is often the hardest lesson to learn during the waiting season, but it is also one of the most rewarding. Just as a farmer patiently waits for his crops to grow, so we must wait for God's perfect plan to unfold in our lives. Through our prayers and patience, we learned that waiting was not a time to be idle but a time to grow in faith, trust, and character.

For you, cultivating patience is about trusting that God is working behind the scenes, even when you cannot see the fruit yet. It is about understanding that His timing is better than your own, and He is preparing you for what's to come.

A PRAYER FOR YOU

Heavenly Father, help me to cultivate patience during this waiting season. Teach me to trust in Your perfect timing and to rest in the knowledge that You are working on my behalf. Give me the strength to be patient as I wait for the fruit of Your promises. In Jesus' name, Amen.

AN INTROSPECTIVE ACTION

Identify a situation in your life where you need to practice patience. Whether it is with your current mate or your future spouse, ask God to help you develop patience in that area. Reflect on how patience builds your faith and character.

A MEDITATIVE THOUGHT

Reflect on James 5:7, *"Be patient therefore, brethren, unto the coming of the Lord. Behold, the husbandman waiteth for the precious fruit of the earth, and hath long patience for it, until he receives the early and latter rain,"* and the image of a farmer waiting for his crops to grow. Trust that the waiting process is necessary for growth and fruitfulness. Allow this meditation to deepen your patience as you wait for God to move.

UP CLOSE & PERSONAL

Strength for the Season You Are in. Your journey may include hands that have never worn a ring, once removed one, or now treasure one as a keepsake. Know this: God is strengthening you for the season you're in. You may not see all He's doing, but He is building resilience, endurance, and deeper trust within you. Your story is not on hold, it's being refined. He hasn't forgotten you. He's fortifying your heart so that when love comes again, you'll be ready, not just to receive it, but to sustain it with God-given strength.

> *"God is not just preparing your future; He is preparing you to stand strong in it."*

JOURNAL YOUR THOUGHTS

DAY 14

ALIGNING YOUR DESIRES WITH GOD'S WILL

SCRIPTURE

"Delight thyself also in the Lord; and he shall give thee the desires of thine heart."
(Psalm 37:4)

JOURNEY OF LOVE AND DEVOTION

When we look back at our journey towards meeting each other, we see how much our desires shifted the more we sought God. Initially, our desires were about finding someone who met our personal checklists, but as we spent more time in prayer, our hearts began to align with God's will.

God does not just give us what we desire, He refines our desires. As we delight in Him, He molds our hearts to desire the things He has for us. The key is to trust that God knows what's best and that His desires for us are far greater than what we could imagine on our own.

For you, aligning your desires with God's will means trusting that His plans for your life are better than anything you could create for yourself. Delight in Him and watch how He fills your heart with desires that align with His perfect will.

A PRAYER FOR YOU

Heavenly Father, help me to align my desires with Yours. I want to delight in You above all else and trust that Your will is the best for my life. Shape my heart to desire what You desire and help me to trust that You will bring the right person into my life in Your perfect timing. In Jesus' name, Amen.

AN INTROSPECTIVE ACTION

Write down three desires you currently hold in your heart, whether relational, personal, or spiritual. Then, beside each one, ask: *"Is this aligned with God's will, or just my own will?"* Invite the Holy Spirit to refine your motives and surrender each desire in prayer, trusting God to shape them according to His perfect plan.

A MEDITATIVE THOUGHT

Selah. Meditate on Psalm 37:4, *"Delight thyself also in the Lord; and he shall give thee the desires of thine heart."* Picture yourself delighting in the Lord, not for what He can give you, but simply for who He is. As you spend time in His presence, trust that your desires are being transformed to reflect His heart. Rest in the peace that comes from alignment—where your deepest longings meet His perfect will.

UP CLOSE & PERSONAL

Aligning Your Desires with God's Will. Your nights may be spent in solitude, in silent ache, or with sacred memories beside you, this devotion gently invites you to realign your heart. Your story still matters to God. He sees every longing and hears every silent hope. But more than granting your desires, He wants to shape them, so they reflect His best for you. Trust that as you delight in Him, He is not only preparing your future but purifying your desires to match His perfect will. In that alignment, true fulfillment is found.

> *"God does not just give desires.*
> *He shapes them first."*

JOURNAL YOUR THOUGHTS

_____

_____

_____

_____

_____

_____

_____

_____

DAY 15
STRENGTH IN WAITING

SCRIPTURE

"The Lord is good unto them that wait for him, to the soul that seeketh him. It is good that a man should both hope and quietly wait for the salvation of the Lord."
(Lamentations 3:25-26)

JOURNEY OF LOVE AND DEVOTION

Waiting is not just about sitting idly—it is about finding strength in the process. During our 33 combined years of prayer, we learned that there was strength to be found in the waiting. The waiting season was not wasted, it was the time God used to refine us, shape us, and prepare our wills for each other.

While we wait on the Heavenly Father, we are actively seeking Him. It is during this time of seeking that God reveals His plans to us. His timing may not align with our own, but He is good, and He will make all things beautiful in His time.

For you, remember that waiting is not a passive experience. It is an opportunity to deepen your relationship with God, to grow in faith, and to prepare for the beautiful future He has for you.

A PRAYER FOR YOU

Heavenly Father, help me to find strength in my waiting. Teach me to actively seek You during this season, trusting that You are good and that You have a plan for my life. Give me the patience to wait for Your perfect timing quietly and to trust that You are working on my behalf. In Jesus' name, Amen.

AN INTROSPECTIVE ACTION

Reflect on your current waiting season and make a list of three things you are currently waiting on. Are you waiting passively or actively seeking God? Take time today to pray, asking God to strengthen you in your waiting. Ask Him to help you find peace and strength to surrender each item to Him as you trust in His timing.

A MEDITATIVE THOUGHT

Pause and Reflect on Lamentations 3:25–26, *"The Lord is good unto them that wait for him, to the soul that seeketh him. It is good that a man should both hope and quietly wait for the salvation of the Lord."* Sit with the truth; *it is good to quietly wait for the Lord.* Inhale peace, exhale frustration. Trust that God's timing is not only perfect, it is protective. Let Him be your strength today.

UP CLOSE & PERSONAL

Strength in Waiting. If you're in a waiting season for healing, restoration, or love, take heart: God is strengthening you even now. Your waiting is not punishment, it's preparation. He sees the end from the beginning, and He is using this time to get you ready for what's next. Trust Him. The strength you gain in this season will carry you into the one you've been praying for. Trust that His timing is perfect, and your love story is unfolding exactly as He designed.

> *"God's timing is not a delay; it's a divine design for your good."*

JOURNAL YOUR THOUGHTS

_____

_____

_____

_____

_____

_____

_____

_____

DAY 16
EMBRACING GOD'S TIMING

SCRIPTURE

"To everything there is a season, and a time to every purpose under the heaven."
(Ecclesiastes 3:1)

JOURNEY OF LOVE AND DEVOTION

There is something sacred about surrendering to God's timing. In our journey, we did not always understand the delays or the quiet seasons, but we chose to believe that God was weaving something beautiful, even in the waiting.

We often returned to the altar of prayer with questions, hopes, and surrendered timelines. What we found was peace, not because everything made sense, but because His presence met us there. Waiting was not a punishment; it was preparation. God was working in the deep places of our hearts, aligning us not only for each other but for the purpose He had designed for our union.

To embrace God's timing is to let go of the need to control the outcome. It is to trust that what He builds in secret will one day bloom in the open, right on time.

So, if you find yourself in the in-between, keep praying. Keep trusting. Keep yielding. God's timing is never late, it is layered with wisdom, mercy, and love. Let Him lead you and know that what He is preparing for you is worth every moment of surrender.

A PRAYER FOR YOU

Heavenly Father, I surrender the pressure I have placed on time. Teach me to rest in Your peace, not my own. Remind me that every delay has a purpose, and every season holds your hand. Help me release anxiety and embrace the quiet confidence that You are preparing something far better than I could imagine. Help me to wait with hope, knowing that You are working all things for my good. In Jesus' name, Amen.

AN INTROSPECTIVE ACTION

Think of one area in your life where you feel like God is taking "too long." Write it down. Now, beneath it, write what you believe God might be teaching or growing in you during this season. Close your journal entry with a short prayer of release, surrendering your timeline to Him. Now give God thanks as you embrace the season you are in.

A MEDITATIVE THOUGHT

Meditate on the idea that there is a season for everything. Trust that your waiting season has a purpose and that God is using this time to prepare you for the future He has planned. Slowly read Ecclesiastes 3:1, *"To everything there is a season, and a time to every purpose under the heaven."* Know this: Each season of your life is necessary, not wasted.

UP CLOSE & PERSONAL

Embracing God's Timing. Whether you're waiting for love, grieving what was, or wondering if it will ever come again, remember this: God's timing is rooted in love, not delay. The season you're in is not a detour, it's preparation. Trust that the God who sees the end from the beginning is guiding your steps with wisdom, grace, and perfect timing. He is faithful, and what He's preparing for you is worth the wait.

> *"Whatever feels like a delay is often a divine alignment in disguise."*

JOURNAL YOUR THOUGHTS

_____

_____

_____

_____

_____

_____

_____

_____

DAY 17
PATIENCE IN PREPARATION

SCRIPTURE

"But let patience have her perfect work, that ye may be perfect and entire, wanting nothing."
(James 1:4)

JOURNEY OF LOVE AND DEVOTION

Patience is not just about waiting—it is about being *made ready* by the hand of God. Before we ever crossed paths, we were in separate seasons of preparation. And though those seasons stretched us, challenged us, and even broke us in places, they were necessary. God was not just answering our prayers, He was refining us through them.

Looking back, we see now how God was working in the quiet, shaping our hearts to reflect His. He was removing the residue of past wounds, restoring confidence, and drawing us deeper into His presence. We were not waiting aimlessly—we were being made whole in Him, so that when the time came, we could step into His promise fully and faithfully.

For you, this time is sacred. Let God prepare you. Let Him mold your character, mature your faith, and align your heart with His. Trust that He is doing the same for the one He is preparing for you. This season is a divine development. Patience, in God's hands, becomes preparation for the promise.

A PRAYER FOR YOU

Heavenly Father, help me to see this waiting season as a time of preparation. Give me the patience to trust that You are working in my heart and life to prepare me for the future You have for me. Help me to become the person You want me to be. In Jesus' name, Amen.

AN INTROSPECTIVE ACTION

Take time today to reflect on how God may be preparing your mind in this season. Write down areas where you feel God is working in your life. Pray for strength as He prepares you for the future.

A MEDITATIVE THOUGHT

Reflect on James 1:4, *"But let patience have her perfect work, that ye may be perfect and entire, wanting nothing."* Allow it to sink in that your patience is refining you. Trust that God is using this time to make you whole, so you will be ready for the person He has chosen for you.

UP CLOSE & PERSONAL

Patience in Preparation. Whether you're praying for love, recovering from loss, or uncertain if your heart will open again, know this: God's timing is never careless. It's rooted in love, layered with purpose, and designed for your good. This season isn't a pause in your story; it's part of His plan. Even when you can't see it, by God's divine providence, He is aligning the right moments, the right people, and the right opportunities. Trust the God who writes endings from the beginning. He is faithful, and what He's preparing for you will be worth every surrendered moment of patience.

> *God is not withholding He's wisely preparing what your heart will be ready to receive in due season.*

JOURNAL YOUR THOUGHTS

_____
_____
_____
_____
_____
_____
_____
_____
_____
_____
_____
_____

DAY 18
TRUSTING IN GOD'S SOVEREIGNTY

SCRIPTURE

"There are many devices in a man's heart; nevertheless, the counsel of the Heavenly Father, that shall stand."
(Proverbs 19:21)

JOURNEY OF LOVE AND DEVOTION

We trusted that God was in control of our journey, even when the road ahead did not make sense. From the very beginning, it was clear that our meeting was not random, it was divinely timed. The way our paths crossed, the prayers that aligned before we ever knew each other… it could only be God. His hand was in every detail.

God's sovereignty means that nothing about your story is random. Every disappointment, every delay, and every breakthrough are part of a masterpiece that only He can see in full. That is the beauty of God's sovereignty, He sees what we cannot. He orchestrates what we could never plan. And even when life feels uncertain, He remains steady, faithful, and sovereign over it all.

For you, trusting in God's sovereignty is a sacred surrender. It is placing your future in the hands of the One who holds time itself. It is choosing to believe that even when you do not see the full picture, He's already painting it with love and purpose. Rest in that truth. What God has planned will never be shaken.

A PRAYER FOR YOU

Heavenly Father, help me to trust in Your sovereignty. I give You the details of my life and my future spouse, trusting that You are in control. Guide me in Your perfect will and help me to rest in the certainty that Your plans for me are good. In Jesus' name, Amen.

AN INTROSPECTIVE ACTION

Set aside time today to write a "release letter" to God. Include dreams, timelines, or unanswered questions weighing on your heart. One by one, surrender each to His control. Then, read Proverbs 19:21 aloud and declare: "God's counsel over my life will stand." Keep this letter as a reminder to trust Him when fear or impatience rises.

A MEDITATIVE THOUGHT

Reflect on Proverbs 19:21, *"There are many devices in a man's heart; nevertheless, the counsel of the Heavenly Father, that shall stand."* Reflect on God's sovereignty. Trust that He is guiding your life, your steps, and your relationship journey, even when you cannot see the full plan. Release the urge to figure it all out and simply trust the One who already has.

UP CLOSE & PERSONAL

Trusting in God's Sovereignty. Love can be something you have yet to experience, have painfully released, or once held but had to let go. Take heart, God is not just watching your story unfold, He's writing it. His sovereignty guarantees that no detail is missed, no prayer is wasted, and no season is outside His control. You don't have to see the full picture to trust the One holding the brush. Rest in His authority. Release your plans. And rejoice that His counsel over your life *will* stand.

> *"God's sovereignty does not require you to understand... just your trust."*

JOURNAL YOUR THOUGHTS

_____
_____
_____
_____
_____
_____
_____
_____
_____

DAY 19
GUARDING YOUR HEART

SCRIPTURE

"Keep thy heart with all diligence; for out of it are the issues of life."
(Proverbs 4:23)

JOURNEY OF LOVE AND DEVOTION

During our waiting season, we learned the sacred discipline of guarding our hearts. It was not always easy. Desire has a voice, and emotions can be loud. But in prayer, God began to teach us the difference between being open and being led and how to yield our hearts to Him, not our feelings.

Guarding our hearts did not mean shutting down; it meant tuning in to God's voice, His timing, and His peace. It meant letting His wisdom lead, rather than our own understanding or emotional urgency. In doing so, we learned to trust that His boundaries were a form of protection and preparation.

For you, guarding your heart is a form of worship. It is choosing to honor what God is doing in your life by refusing to settle for anything less than His best. It means filtering your thoughts, emotions, and desires through the lens of His Word and His Spirit. When your heart is guarded in Him, it becomes a sacred place for His will to take root and flourish.

A PRAYER FOR YOU

Heavenly Father, help me to guard my heart during this season. Let my emotions be anchored in Your truth, not tossed by temporary feelings. Close every door that leads to distraction, deception, or delay. Show me how to protect the sacred space within me where You dwell. Give me wisdom to make decisions that honor You and protect my future. In Jesus' name, Amen.

AN INTROSPECTIVE ACTION

Take inventory of your emotional life. Are there people, conversations, fantasies, or habits that leave your heart vulnerable to discouragement, distraction, or compromise? List them honestly. Then, one by one, ask the Holy Spirit to give you a strategy for guarding your heart in each area, whether it's establishing a boundary, stepping back from a situation, or replacing unhealthy patterns with prayer and truth. End by writing a declaration: *"My heart belongs to God, and I will guard it with diligence."*

A MEDITATIVE THOUGHT

Selah. Breathe in the promise of God's protection. Reflect deeply on Proverbs 4:23, *"Keep thy heart with all diligence; for out of it are the issues of life."* Picture your heart as a garden—what's being planted there?

What's growing unchecked? Visualize the Holy Spirit standing at the gate, guarding what enters and what remains. As you guard your heart, you are not withholding love, you are preparing to give and receive it from a place of health, holiness, and clarity.

UP CLOSE & PERSONAL

Guarding Your Heart. Maybe your name remained the same, was changed and changed back, or now lives in remembrance; this devotion meets you in your season. Your story still matters to God. He hasn't forgotten you, and He's not late. Continue to guard your heart as He continues to script your love story. Trust that His timing is perfect, and your love story will be complete before you know it.

> Guarding your heart is not fear, it is faith in God's best.

JOURNAL YOUR THOUGHTS

_____

_____

_____

_____

_____

_____

_____

DAY 20
LEARNING TO BE CONTENT

SCRIPTURE

"Not that I speak in respect of want: for I have learned, in whatsoever state I am, therewith to be content. I know both how to be abased, and I know how to abound: every where and in all things I am instructed both to be full and to be hungry, both to abound and to suffer need."
(Philippians 4:11-12)

JOURNEY OF LOVE AND DEVOTION

One of the most transformative lessons we learned in our season of waiting was *contentment*. It did not come overnight, and it certainly was not always easy. But through prayer and surrender, God began to teach us how to rest in Him, right where we were.

Contentment did not mean we stopped hoping or believing. It meant we learned to rejoice *'in the now,'* knowing God was already moving behind the scenes. We found peace in His presence, even before the promise had fully unfolded. Our joy was not rooted in what we lacked, but in the assurance that God was preparing an abundance we could not see.

For you, contentment is a quiet strength. It is the ability to trust that your current season is not a delay, but a design. It is choosing gratitude over frustration, and peace over striving. Let God meet you *'in the now'* and trust that in His perfect timing, *everything* will fall beautifully into place.

A PRAYER FOR YOU

Heavenly Father, teach me the beauty of contentment. Quiet the restless places in my heart and help me to find joy in where You have me right now. Help me to see this season not as something to escape, but as something You are using to shape me. Let me rest in the truth that You are enough. May I be fully present, fully grateful, and fully trusting in You. In Jesus' name, Amen.

AN INTROSPECTIVE ACTION

Take a moment to journal one area where you have been feeling discontent. Beside it, write down a truth from God's Word that speaks peace into that area. Then, list three blessings that are present in your life *right now*, no matter how small. Close by thanking God for what He's already provided and ask Him to continue growing your ability to live with peace, purpose, and contentment in this season.

A MEDITATIVE THOUGHT

Meditate on Philippians 4:11-12, *"Not that I speak in respect of want: for I have learned, in whatsoever state I am, therewith to be content. I know both how to be abased, and I know how to abound everywhere and in all things I am instructed both to be full and to be hungry, both to abound and to suffer need."* Reflect on the idea of being content in every season. Trust that God's provision is more than enough and that He will give you the peace you need in this waiting season.

UP CLOSE & PERSONAL

Learning to be Content. You might be in a season of waiting, a season of rebuilding, or a season of remembering; this is your season to lean into contentment. Contentment doesn't mean you stop hoping; it means you stop striving. It is trusting that God's presence is your portion, even while you wait. Your story still matters to Him. You haven't been overlooked, and you are not behind. His timing is perfect—and in this very moment, He is enough.

> *"Contentment is not the absence of desire; it is the presence of trust."*

JOURNAL YOUR THOUGHTS

_____

_____

_____

_____

_____

_____

DAY 21
TRUSTING GOD'S PLAN

SCRIPTURE

"For I know the thoughts that I think toward you, saith the Heavenly Father, thoughts of peace, and not of evil, to give you an expected end."
(Jeremiah 29:11)

JOURNEY OF LOVE AND DEVOTION

During our waiting season, we each faced moments when our faith was tested. Questions crept in: *Is this still part of God's plan? Did we miss something?* But the more we brought those questions to God in prayer, the more He reminded us: His plan never fails, even when we don't understand the process.

We learned that delays are not rejections, they're redirections. When things didn't happen how or when we thought they would, God was still at work building our trust, aligning our hearts, and preparing something beyond what we had imagined. Over time, we exchanged our expectations for His promises, and we began to rest in the peace of knowing that His ways are always better.

For you, trusting God's plan may mean letting go of the script you've written for your life. It means choosing faith over fear and surrender over striving. His plan may not always match your timeline, but it will always reflect His love, His wisdom, and His glory.

A PRAYER FOR YOU

Heavenly Father, help me to trust Your plans over my own. I surrender my desires to You and trust that You have a purpose in every part of my journey. Guide me as I wait for the future You have for me. Strengthen my heart when the path feels uncertain. Replace my fear with faith and help me rest in Your promise of peace, purpose, and a beautiful end. In Jesus' name, Amen.

AN INTROSPECTIVE ACTION

Take a moment to write down one area of your life where you've been trying to control the outcome. Then, write a short prayer releasing that area to God. Reflect on how trying to control this area has affected your peace. Commit to checking that space daily, praying over it, and reminding yourself that God is in control and working it out for your good.

A MEDITATIVE THOUGHT

Sit and reflect with Jeremiah 29:11, *"For I know the thoughts that I think toward you, saith the Heavenly Father, thoughts of peace, and not of evil, to give you an expected end."* Read it slowly and aloud. Let the words *"expected end"* settle in your heart. Close your eyes and imagine God lovingly weaving the threads of your story into a design you may not yet understand, but one that is filled with peace, purpose, and hope. Your trust grows stronger when you rest in the truth that He already sees the finished work.

UP CLOSE & PERSONAL

Trusting God's Plan. Maybe you're navigating singleness, recovering from heartache, or honoring a love that once was; this season is still part of God's plan. Your life is not off course. His plan includes every moment, even the ones that feel uncertain. Trust that what He's writing is worth surrendering your pen. His plan is not delayed, and neither is your destiny. Rest in the assurance that your story is safe in the hands of the One who sees the end from the beginning and calls it good.

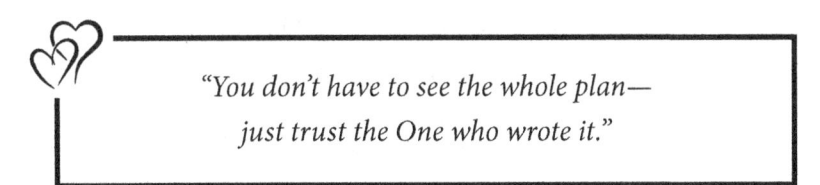

> *"You don't have to see the whole plan—
> just trust the One who wrote it."*

JOURNAL YOUR THOUGHTS

_____

_____

_____

_____

_____

DAY 22

PREPARING YOUR HEART FOR A RELATIONSHIP

SCRIPTURE

*"Create in me a clean heart, O God;
and renew a right spirit within me."*
(Psalm 51:10)

JOURNEY OF LOVE AND DEVOTION

We each had to spend sacred time preparing our hearts for the relationship God was orchestrating. This preparation was not about changing who we were to fit a mold, it was about becoming whole in God first. As we drew closer to Him, He gently shaped us into people who could love from a place of strength, not lack; of wholeness, not need.

This heart work was quiet and often unseen. It meant allowing God to reveal what needed healing, strengthen what felt weak, and build up the qualities that would one day sustain our Covenant: faith, emotional maturity, integrity, and character rooted in Him.

For you, this time is an invitation to go deeper. Let God prepare you inwardly for what He's preparing outwardly. As you grow closer to Him, you become the kind of mate who does not just desire a godly relationship, you are ready to nurture one. Your heart, fully surrendered and refined in His presence, is the foundation for everything beautiful that's to come.

A PRAYER FOR YOU

Heavenly Father, prepare my heart to love Your way. Search me and show me any area where healing, forgiveness, or growth is still needed. Teach me to love myself the way You love me, so that I can one day love someone else with patience, humility, and grace. Purify my motives. Renew my thoughts. Do the work in me that only You can do. In Jesus' name, Amen.

AN INTROSPECTIVE ACTION

Spend 15 quiet minutes reflecting on what you want to bring into a future relationship and what you need to leave behind. Write a list of character traits or emotional habits God may be prompting you to grow in (e.g., patience, self-control, healing from past trauma). Choose one area to focus on this week. Then, write a prayer asking God to develop that part of your heart in preparation for your godly relationship.

A MEDITATIVE THOUGHT

Reflect on Psalm 51:10, *"Create in me a clean heart, O God; and renew a right spirit within me."* Allow God to shape your heart. Ask Him to help you focus on developing inner beauty that will honor Him and strengthen your future relationship.

UP CLOSE & PERSONAL

Preparing Your Heart for a Relationship. Whether you've never been married, are recovering from loss, or healing from heartbreak, know this: you are not waiting in vain. This season is not about passivity, it's about preparation. As God shapes your heart, He is not only preparing you for love; He is protecting the future He's designed for you. Your story still matters. You are not forgotten, and you are not behind. You are being groomed for something real, holy, and worth the wait.

> *"The healthiest relationships begin with hearts already whole in God."*

JOURNAL YOUR THOUGHTS

DAY 23
EMBRACING EMOTIONAL HEALING

SCRIPTURE

"He healeth the broken in heart, and bindeth up their wounds."
(Psalm 14:73)

JOURNEY OF LOVE AND DEVOTION

We did not walk into our relationship whole, we walked in healing. Both of us carried past hurts, silent wounds, and memories that left their mark. But God, in His mercy, did not leave us broken. As we surrendered our pain to Him, He began a gentle, powerful work of restoration.

Emotional healing is not a one-time moment, it is a sacred journey. It required us to be vulnerable before God, to trust Him with the tender places we tried to hide. But in that surrender, He met us with grace. And slowly, surely, He healed what we thought might always ache.

For you, this season may be the doorway to healing. Let God into the places you have protected. He does not just want you to find love, He wants you to be *free* to love, unburdened by yesterday. As He restores you, He's also preparing you to receive the kind of love that reflects His heart. One built not on brokenness, but on healing and hope.

A PRAYER FOR YOU

Heavenly Father, I surrender my emotional wounds to You. Heal my broken heart and bind up my wounds. Help me to release past hurts, so that I can enter into a future relationship with a heart full of love and trust. In Jesus' name, Amen.

AN INTROSPECTIVE ACTION

Reflect on any past emotional wounds that may need healing. Write them down and surrender them to God. Ask Him for healing and peace in those areas, trusting and knowing with all your heart that He is restoring you.

A MEDITATIVE THOUGHT

Sit and reflect on Psalm 14:73, *"He healeth the broken in heart, and bindeth up their wounds."* Allow God to heal your heart. Trust that He is actively working in your life to bring healing and restoration, making you whole in preparation for your future.

UP CLOSE & PERSONAL

Embracing Emotional Healing. Whether you've never been married, are carrying the weight of a painful divorce, or holding onto the sacred memory of a love that once was, this devotion meets you in the deep places of your heart. Emotional healing is not a sign of weakness; it's an invitation to wholeness. Your tears have not gone unnoticed, and your story still matters deeply to God. He is not finished with you. He's gently restoring what was broken and renewing your hope for what's to come. Trust that even in your healing, He is weaving beauty and redeeming your next chapter.

> *"Healing is not the end of your story—it's the beginning of a stronger, more surrendered you."*

JOURNAL YOUR THOUGHTS

_____

_____

_____

_____

_____

_____

_____

_____

_____

_____

_____

_____

_____

_____

_____

DAY 24
THE POWER OF FAITH IN WAITING

SCRIPTURE

"Now faith is the substance of things hoped for, the evidence of things not seen."
(Hebrews 11:1)

JOURNEY OF LOVE AND DEVOTION

Waiting is not just about time, it is about trust. In our season of waiting, no road signs were pointing to what was next. No lightning bolts, no guarantees, just a quiet faith that God was weaving something good behind the veil of what we couldn't yet see.

Faith became more than a belief. It became a posture. We had to let go of our need for control and embrace the unseen hand of God guiding each step. It wasn't easy, but it was holy. Faith reminded us that God doesn't require sight to be present, and He doesn't require answers to be trusted.

If you're in a season where your heart is waiting for a first-time husband, another love, or a new beginning, know this: faith is your power. It anchors you when feelings falter. It lifts your hope when logic fails. And it assures you that what God has promised, He is faithful to perform, right on time.

A PRAYER FOR YOU

Heavenly Father, I thank You that faith is not about having all the answers, but about trusting in Your perfect presence. Strengthen me when doubt tries to whisper louder than truth. Help me to hold onto what You've said, even when I don't yet see it. Increase my faith to believe in the beauty of Your timing and the power of Your plan. Let my heart rest not in outcomes, but in the confidence that You are always working for my good. In Jesus' name, Amen.

AN INTROSPECTIVE ACTION

Write down one area of your life where you feel stuck in waiting. Then, beneath it, write one truth from God's Word that speaks hope into that area. Speak it aloud as a declaration of faith. Each day this week, return to that verse and pray it back to God. Let it shape your thinking and stir your hope. Waiting becomes powerful when it's fueled by faith.

A MEDITATIVE THOUGHT

Take a moment to reflect on Hebrews 11:1, *"Now faith is the substance of things hoped for, the evidence of things not seen."* Breathe in the peace that comes from trusting the unseen hand of God. Picture yourself handing over your questions and expectations to Him. Let your soul rest in knowing that He is not late, not distant, and not unsure. He's moving, preparing, aligning, and your faith is the bridge between the now and the not-yet.

UP CLOSE & PERSONAL

The Power of Faith in Waiting. You may still be waiting to meet someone, healing from love that was lost, or learning to hope again—faith is your companion. God hasn't forgotten your story. He's still writing it, even in the silence. Don't let the waiting weaken your faith; let it deepen it. Trust that His timing is rooted in love and His delays are rich with purpose. Stand firm. Believe boldly. What you cannot yet see is already known to God, and He is faithful to fulfill every word He's spoken over your life.

> *"Faith does not shorten the wait—it strengthens you to endure it with hope."*

JOURNAL YOUR THOUGHTS

_____

_____

_____

_____

_____

_____

_____

_____

_____

DAY 25
EXPECTING GOD'S BEST

SCRIPTURE

"And we know that all things work together for good to them that love God, to them who are the called according to His purpose."
(Romans 8:28)

JOURNEY OF LOVE AND DEVOTION

One of the most powerful decisions we made during our journey was to expect God's best. Not because everything looked promising on the surface, but because we trusted the character of the God we serve. Expectation is not entitlement, it's anchored faith.

There were days we had to silence doubt and remind ourselves that God's best might not always come packaged in the way we imagined, but it would always be what we needed, when we needed it. That shift in mindset brought peace and joy even in the waiting.

For you, expecting God's best means refusing to settle. It means believing you are deeply loved, fully seen, and purposefully prepared. It's trusting that God is not delaying to disappoint you but positioning you to receive what aligns with His divine purpose for your life. Keep your heart open, your hope alive, and your faith rooted in the One who always delivers on His promises.

A PRAYER FOR YOU

Heavenly Father, I choose today to expect Your best. Not because I deserve it, but because I trust that You are a good Father who delights in giving good gifts to Your children. Help me to release every fear of disappointment and embrace the truth that You are working all things together for my good. Align my desires with Your will, and strengthen me with faith as I wait with joyful expectation. In Jesus' name, Amen.

AN INTROSPECTIVE ACTION

Reflect on the things you want in a future mate. Write down your top five desires in a future relationship, not just outward traits, but spiritual, emotional, and character-based hopes. Beside each one, write a short prayer that invites God to share with you in those same areas. Then, pray that God will provide exactly what you need. Trust that He will give you His best.

A MEDITATIVE THOUGHT

Reflect on Romans 8:28, *"And we know that all things work together for good to them that love God, to them who are the called according to His purpose."* Allow this truth to settle in your heart. Now imagine God's hands gently weaving all those threads together into something purposeful. As you meditate, say aloud: *"God is working this for my good and His best is on the way."* Let your heart rest in that truth.

UP CLOSE & PERSONAL

Expecting God's Peace. You may have never given your heart away, once had it broken, or still feel it beat for someone now in eternity. This is your invitation to expect again. Your story still matters to God. He hasn't forgotten you, and He's not finished. What He's preparing for you is not second-best, it's sacred, set apart, and worth the wait. Expect God's best, not because of what you see, but because of who He is.

> "God's best is worth the wait, the healing, and the preparation it requires."

JOURNAL YOUR THOUGHTS

DAY 26
PREPARING FOR MARRIAGE IN SPIRIT

SCRIPTURE

"Husbands, love your wives, even as Christ also loved the church, and gave Himself for it."
(Ephesians 5:25)

JOURNEY OF LOVE AND DEVOTION

Before we ever met, we each made a decision to prepare our hearts for more than just a relationship, we prepared for *covenant*. We knew that a Christ-centered marriage required more than love; it required spiritual readiness. So, we turned inward and upward, letting God do the heart work that would one day sustain our union.

We spent time in prayer, in the Word, and in reflection. We asked God to shape us into the kind of mate who could love selflessly, forgive quickly, and walk humbly. We were not just waiting for someone else to show up—we were becoming the person someone else had been praying for.

For you, this season is sacred preparation. Let God align your heart with His will. Let Him cultivate within you the fruits that will flourish in a godly marriage: patience, kindness, wisdom, and grace. Preparing for marriage is not about perfection, it is about becoming whole in Christ, so that when the time comes, you can love from a place of strength, not striving.

A PRAYER FOR YOU

Heavenly Father, help me to prepare my heart and spirit for the marriage You have for me. Teach me to love selflessly, to grow in my relationship with You, and to become the person You have called me to be. In Jesus' name, Amen.

AN INTROSPECTIVE ACTION

Pause for a moment and think about how you can grow spiritually to prepare for marriage. Ask God to show you areas where you can develop as a mate, write them down, and pray for wisdom and strength in this preparation process.

A MEDITATIVE THOUGHT

Reflect on Ephesians 5:25, *"Husbands, love your wives, even as Christ also loved the church, and gave Himself for it."* Reflect on the kind of love God calls us to have in marriage. Pray for the ability to love selflessly, just as Christ loves the church.

UP CLOSE & PERSONAL

Preparing for Marriage in Spirit. Maybe you are entering into love for the first time, walking away from something that once was, or walking with a memory tucked inside. This is your season to prepare in spirit.

Marriage begins long before the wedding; it begins in the heart, in private surrender, and in spiritual alignment with God's will. Your story still matters deeply to Him. He has not forgotten you, and He is not done preparing you. What He is shaping within you now is not just for a relationship, it is for purpose. Prepare with expectation. Grow in faith. Let God do the inner work so you can step into covenant ready, whole, and spiritually grounded in His design.

> *"Preparing for marriage begins with surrender, not strategy."*

JOURNAL YOUR THOUGHTS

_____
_____
_____
_____
_____
_____
_____
_____
_____
_____
_____
_____

DAY 27
LIVING IN EXPECTATION

SCRIPTURE

"Blessed are those servants, whom the lord when he cometh shall find watching: verily I say unto you, that he shall gird himself, and make them to sit down to meat, and will come forth and serve them."
(Luke 12:37)

JOURNEY OF LOVE AND DEVOTION

We lived with a quiet, steady expectation that God would bring our relationship to life in His perfect timing. It was not wishful thinking—it was faith in action. Every prayer we prayed, every step we took, was grounded in the belief that God was moving, even when we could not yet see the evidence.

Expectation, for us, was not passive. It was active trust. It meant preparing our hearts, guarding our hope, and aligning our lives with what we believed God had spoken. We did not know *when* the promise would unfold, but we lived like it would. And in His faithfulness,

God met that expectation with something far more beautiful than we imagined.

For you, living in expectation is a sacred posture. It is holding hope close, even in the waiting. It is trusting that God is not only able—but willing—to fulfill what He has promised. Prepare your heart with faith. Keep walking in readiness. What God has planned for you is already unfolding behind the scenes.

A PRAYER FOR YOU

Heavenly Father, teach me how to wait with joyful expectation. Strengthen my faith in the quiet spaces where nothing seems to be moving. Help me prepare with purpose, not fear. Shape my mindset to believe that what You've spoken will come to pass. I surrender my timeline and choose to walk in step with You, trusting that Your best is on its way. Let my attitude reflect my hope. Let my faith be steady, and my heart remain open to every good thing You have planned. In Jesus' name, Amen.

AN INTROSPECTIVE ACTION

Reflect on your expectations for the future. Are you living in hope and trust that God is going to provide what you need? Pray for the strength to live with anticipation of God's plan.

A MEDITATIVE THOUGHT

Reflect on Luke 12:37, *"Blessed are those servants, whom the lord when he cometh shall find watching: verily I say unto you, that he shall gird himself, and make them to sit down to meat, and will come forth and serve them."* Reflect on the joy of being ready and expectant for God's move in your life. Imagine it. Now, walk in it.

UP CLOSE & PERSONAL

Living in Expectation. Your story may be just beginning, being rewritten, or resting gently in God's eternal hands; this season calls you to wait with hope. Living in expectation is not denial of reality; it's full awareness that God is still writing your story. He hasn't forgotten you, and His plans are not delayed, they're deliberate. Keep your heart lifted. Keep preparing. The fulfillment is coming, and when it does, it will be better than anything you imagined—because it came from Him.

> *"Expectation rooted in faith is preparation wrapped in hope."*

JOURNAL YOUR THOUGHTS

DAY 28
TRUSTING THE PROCESS

SCRIPTURE

"Being confident of this very thing, that he which hath begun a good work in you will perform it until the day of Jesus Christ."
(Philippians 1:6)

JOURNEY OF LOVE AND DEVOTION

We learned that trusting the process really means trusting *God* in every season, every step, every pause. The waiting, the stretching, the unseen growth… none of it was wasted. God was using it all to build something stronger, deeper, and more beautiful for us, individually and as a couple.

There were moments when we wanted to move faster, to see more, to understand why. But in prayer, we discovered that God was doing something eternal in us, not just preparing us for each other, but shaping us for purpose. Trusting the process required surrender. And surrender gave birth to a deeper hope that *God's plan was still unfolding—even in silence.*

For you, trusting the process means laying down your timeline and embracing God's. It means believing that He is working in every moment—seen and unseen—to bring about something holy. The process may be uncomfortable, but it is sacred. Let God write your story, and you will see that every chapter was necessary.

A PRAYER FOR YOU

Heavenly Father, thank You that I am a work in progress, and You are a faithful Creator who never gives up on what You've started. Help me to trust You in the in-between moments; the ones that stretch me and grow me. Give me eyes to see Your hand even when I feel stuck, and faith to believe that this process is preparing me for something purposeful. Teach me to rest in Your rhythm and surrender every unfinished part to Your perfect timing. In Jesus' name, Amen.

AN INTROSPECTIVE ACTION

Take time to reflect on one area of your life where you feel like you are still "in process." Write out how you have seen growth—emotionally, spiritually, or relationally—even if it has been slow. Then, write a declaration of faith: *"God is not done with me, and I will not give up on what He is shaping in me."* Post it somewhere you'll see daily as a reminder that transformation takes time.

A MEDITATIVE THOUGHT

Reflect on Philippians 1:6 and let the words wash over your heart: *He will perform it.* Visualize your life as a canvas that the Master Artist is still painting. The strokes may feel unfinished, but they are intentional. Allow the Holy Spirit to reassure you that this process, however messy or unclear, is sacred and necessary. Trust the Artist. The masterpiece is in progress.

UP CLOSE & PERSONAL

Trusting the Process. You may have spent time waiting, weeping, or whispering farewell, - know this - this season is not a detour; it's divine preparation. Trust that your story still matters to God. He's not finished with you, and the process you're in is part of the promise He's fulfilling. Every waiting moment, every lesson, every surrender is shaping something holy. Let Him finish what He's started, and believe that the outcome will be more beautiful than anything you could have planned.

> *"You are not behind—you are becoming. Trust the God who finishes what He starts."*

JOURNAL YOUR THOUGHTS

_____
_____
_____
_____
_____
_____
_____

DAY 29
WALKING IN BOLDNESS

SCRIPTURE

"For God hath not given us the spirit of fear; but of power, and of love, and of a sound mind."
(2 Timothy 1:7)

JOURNEY OF LOVE AND DEVOTION

We had to learn to walk in boldness, not in our own strength, but in the confidence that comes from knowing God had gone before us. Fear, doubt, and people tried to whisper unbelief along the way, but through prayer, we were reminded that God had already equipped us for the journey ahead.

Boldness did not mean we never felt afraid, it meant we chose faith over fear. We stepped forward, not because we had all the answers, but because we trusted the One who held the blueprint. And with every step, God proved Himself faithful.

For you, walking in boldness means rising above the voices of insecurity and stepping into the truth of who you are in Christ. He has already placed within you everything needed for what lies ahead. Even when the path feels unknown, trust that His Spirit within you is greater. Move forward with courage. Your yes to God activates what He has already prepared for you.

A PRAYER FOR YOU

Heavenly Father, I thank You that You have not given me a spirit of fear. Remind me daily that I am equipped with power, filled with Your love, and guided by a sound mind. Uproot the lies that keep me playing small. Help me to rise with boldness in every area You've called me to: relationships, healing, purpose, and preparation. Let my "yes" to You be louder than my "what ifs." I choose to walk in confidence, not because I have it all figured out, but because I trust the One who does. In Jesus' name, Amen.

AN INTROSPECTIVE ACTION

Write down three areas in your life where fear has kept you from moving forward—emotionally, relationally, or spiritually. For each one, find a scripture (starting with 2 Timothy 1:7) to combat that fear with truth. Then write a bold declaration like: *"I will no longer shrink in this area. God has given me boldness, not fear."* Post it where you can see it and repeat it until your mind aligns with your spirit.

A MEDITATIVE THOUGHT

Reflect on 2 Timothy 1:7, *"For God hath not given us the spirit of fear."* Let each phrase land deeply in your spirit—power... love... sound mind. Envision yourself walking forward into your calling with steady feet and a confident heart. The fear you feel does not come from God. Boldness does. Walk in what He has already placed within you.

UP CLOSE & PERSONAL

Walking in Boldness. No matter where love last found you – never, once, twice, or forever - boldness still belongs to you. God is not calling you to play it safe. He is calling you to rise with courage, to love with strength, and to expect with faith. You are not behind. You are becoming. Walk in boldness, not because the path is easy, but because the Spirit within you is powerful, loving, and steady. Boldness is your birthright in Christ, step into it.

> *"Boldness is walking forward even when the path is unclear."*

JOURNAL YOUR THOUGHTS

_____
_____
_____
_____
_____
_____
_____

DAY 30
BUILT BY THE LORD

SCRIPTURE

"Except the Lord build the house, they labour in vain that build it."
(Psalm 127:1)

JOURNEY OF LOVE AND DEVOTION

As we close this devotional, we do so with hearts overflowing with gratitude. Not just for the story God wrote for us, but for the *foundation* He built it upon PRAYER. Every step of our journey, every decision, every moment of waiting and wondering, was strengthened by the time we spent on our knees.

A foundation built on prayer is not just a starting point—it is a lifeline. It is what steadied us in uncertainty, sustained us in silence, and aligned our hearts with God's perfect will. Prayer shaped our individual paths and ultimately knit them together. It was never about eloquent words—it was about open hearts, surrendered spirits, and a deep longing to hear from God.

We are living proof that when you follow God's direction and trust in His promises, *He will never leave you.* His presence is not only with you—it goes before you, prepares the way, and surrounds you with peace.

For you, let prayer be more than a request—it is the place where intimacy with God is formed, where trust is built, and where His voice becomes your guide. Let it be your foundation. Because anything built apart from prayer may shake, but what is built on prayer will stand.

You are not alone. God is with you—guiding, comforting, preparing, and unfolding a plan far greater than you can imagine. Let His presence be your promise. Let His voice be your anchor. And let your foundation always be built on prayer.

A PRAYER FOR YOU

Heavenly Father, thank You for seeing me, loving me, and holding my future in Your hands. In this season of singleness, help me to build my life on the unshakable foundation of prayer. Teach me to seek You first, not just for a spouse, but for deeper intimacy with You. Let my waiting be filled with worship, my hope anchored in faith, and my foundation firmly planted in You. In Jesus' name, Amen.

AN INTROSPECTIVE ACTION

Set aside 10 minutes today to pray intentionally over your future. Write down three areas where you want God to strengthen your foundation—whether it is faith, healing, or patience—and lift each one to Him in prayer. Let this moment be a brick in the foundation you are building with Him.

A MEDITATIVE THOUGHT

"Unless the Lord builds the house, they labor in vain who build it," Psalm 127:1. Close your eyes and take a deep breath. Picture your heart as a home under construction—not rushed, not abandoned, but steadily built by God's hand. Feel the strength of each prayer you have whispered while

reading this devotional. Let it become a stone in the foundation. Let go of control. Release your timeline. Invite the Master Builder to continue His work in you. Rest in the truth that what is built on prayer will stand.

UP CLOSE & PERSONAL

Built by the Lord. No matter if you are walking alone, walking away, or walking with grief, know this: you are being built by the Lord. Your story isn't random or forgotten; it's being crafted by the Master Builder who sees every detail and works with eternal precision. He is establishing something lasting in you, something that will not crumble with time or sorrow. Trust that He's laying the foundation, strengthening the framework, and preparing a love story that reflects His glory. You are not just waiting, you are becoming. And what God builds is always worth the process. Invite Him In and He Will Take It From There. Selah!

"If it is built by the Lord, it will not fall."

JOURNAL YOUR THOUGHTS

_____

_____

_____

_____

_____

DAY 31
HEALING AFTER LOVE ENDS

SCRIPTURE

"He restoreth my soul: he leadeth me in the paths of righteousness for his name's sake."
(Psalm 23:3)

JOURNEY OF LOVE AND DEVOTION

There is a quiet kind of grief that comes with divorce. It is the death of a dream, the unraveling of a covenant, and often, the unspoken ache of shame or guilt. But here is the truth we had to learn—even in the places where love was lost, God's love remains.

Divorce was never part of God's original plan, but neither is condemnation. What He offers instead is restoration, the kind that reaches down into your soul and begins to rebuild. We each had to release past versions of ourselves—the ones shaped by fear, unmet expectations, and disappointment. And it was in that releasing that God restored us.

You are not disqualified. You are not discarded. You are deeply loved by a God who specializes in redemption. Let Him lead you through this season—not by the weight of what was, but by the promise of what still can be.

A PRAYER FOR YOU

Heavenly Father, I give You the pieces of my past. Heal the parts of me still wounded by disappointment, betrayal, or regret. I believe You are the God who restores. Lead me gently down paths of righteousness, and help me to trust that what's ahead is greater than what's behind. In Jesus' name, Amen.

AN INTROSPECTIVE ACTION

Write a letter to your past self—the version of you that endured heartbreak or disappointment in your marriage. Offer compassion, truth, and forgiveness. Then write a second letter to your future self, declaring hope and restoration over your next chapter.

A MEDITATIVE THOUGHT

Reflect and let Psalm 23:3 minister to your soul. *"He restoreth my soul: he leadeth me in the paths of righteousness for his name's sake."* Hear Him say, "I restore." You are not broken beyond repair. You are in the hands of a Restorer who knows exactly how to rebuild you—stronger, softer, and surrendered.

UP CLOSE & PERSONAL

Healing After Love Ends. After you've walked through the heartbreak of divorce, know this: healing is holy, and restoration is possible. You are not defined by what ended—you are held by the One who never left. This devotional was written to remind you that even when love has unraveled, God's love weaves something new. He sees every tear, every silent prayer, and every hopeful heartbeat. Let Him heal what was, so you can hope again for what will be.

> *"God does not discard broken things—He rebuilds them into testimonies of grace."*

JOURNAL YOUR THOUGHTS

DAY 32
HONORING LOVE LOST, EMBRACING LOVE AHEAD

SCRIPTURE

"He will swallow up death in victory; and the Lord God will wipe away tears from off all faces…"
(Isaiah 25:8)

JOURNEY OF LOVE AND DEVOTION

Grief has a way of arriving in waves—sometimes expected, sometimes uninvited. And when you have known deep love, the silence left behind can feel unbearable. But even in this silence, God is present. You may have lost a spouse, but you have not lost your capacity to love—or to be loved again.

What you shared was sacred. And God honors that. But He also promises new mercies, fresh oil, and the possibility of joy after sorrow. That doesn't mean forgetting the one you loved—it means embracing the truth that God is not finished with your heart. We believe He can write new chapters without erasing the old ones. He can hold your memories in one hand and your future in the other. And we believe He will wipe every tear, just as He promises.

PRAYER FOR YOU

Heavenly Father, Thank You for the gift of love I have experienced. Today, I invite You into the tender places of grief. I honor the one I've lost, but I also open my heart to the possibility of love again. Heal me. Hold me. Lead me into hope. In Jesus' name, Amen.

AN INTROSPECTIVE ACTION

Sit with a photo, memento, or memory of the one you loved. Say their name aloud and thank God for the gift they were. Then, prayerfully write down one way you sense God inviting you to hope again. It could be a conversation, a trip, a prayer, or simply being open to love in a new form. Honor the past. Permit God to lead your heart forward.

A MEDITATIVE THOUGHT

Get in a quiet place and reflect on Isaiah 25:8, *"He will swallow up death in victory; and the Lord God will wipe away tears from off all faces...."* See the Lord drawing near to your sorrow, wiping your tears with care. Let His presence bring comfort and courage. Grief and joy can walk together. God holds space for both, and He holds space for you.

UP CLOSE & PERSONAL

Honoring Love Lost, Embracing Love Ahead. Maybe you're grieving the loss of a spouse, carrying the memories of a love that once was, or wondering if your heart could ever open again—this devotion meets you here. God sees every tear and honors every moment you've shared. But He also holds new beginnings in His hands. Your story still matters to Him. He is not finished with your heart, and He is not late. Trust that even in the ache, His love is writing something beautiful ahead.

> "God holds space for your memories and your future—He's not finished with your heart."

JOURNAL YOUR THOUGHTS

_____

_____

_____

_____

_____

_____

_____

_____

_____

_____

_____

_____

_____

_____

DAY 33
COME: LET THE AUTHOR WRITE YOUR STORY

SCRIPTURE

"Look unto me, and be ye saved, all the ends of the earth: for I am God, and there is none else."
(Isaiah 45:22)

A JOURNEY OF LOVE AND DEVOTION

There comes a moment when we realize that no matter how much we try to shape our own story, something is still missing. The love we're seeking, the security we long for, the peace we crave—they're not found in people, plans, or perfection. They're found in a Person. His name is Jesus.

Spiritual and emotional guardianship begins with one powerful act: surrender. When you don't know where to turn, He simply says, *"Look unto Me."* He is not asking you to fix yourself before coming. He's asking you to trust Him to do the work. Your heart is not too broken. Your past is not too complicated. Your future is not too far gone.

When you give your heart to the One who made it, He doesn't just hold it—He heals it. He guards it. He leads it. He writes a story filled with redemption, restoration, and true love. His arms are stretched wide open, saying, *"Come."*

A PRAYER FOR YOU

Heavenly Father, I have tried to carry my own heart, but today I realize I need You. I need Your love, Your protection, and Your guidance. I give You my past, my pain, my dreams—and ask You to begin again. Be the Author of my life, the Guardian of my emotions, and the Keeper of my soul. Teach me how to walk in healing, how to wait with hope, and how to love with wholeness. Thank You for loving me before I even knew how to love You. Today, I respond to Your invitation and say, *"Here I am. Write my story."* In Jesus' name, Amen.

AN INTROSPECTIVE ACTION

Find a quiet space and write a letter to God. If you've never talked to Him before, begin with: *"God, if You are real and You care, I want to know You."* Be honest. Share your fears, longings, and regrets. Then, ask Him to begin the work of healing and to reveal Himself to you. Seal this moment by writing, *"I give You permission to write my story."* Save the letter—it will become a powerful reminder of where your new journey began.

A MEDITATIVE THOUGHT

Stop, sit, read slowly ... now read it again, Isaiah 45:22, *"Look unto Me, and be ye saved..."* Close your eyes and imagine God extending His hand toward you. You don't have to strive. You don't have to fix it all. Just look to Him. As you look, surrender the pressure to figure everything out.

Let His love quiet your heart and awaken your hope. He's not far away. He's near—and He's waiting.

FINAL PARAGRAPH FOR THE SEEKING, THE DIVORCED, AND THE WIDOWED

For the one who's NEVER KNOWN HIM, but longs for love:

You do not have to search in the dark anymore. The One who created you is calling you into a relationship, not just with another person, but with Himself. His arms are stretched wide open, saying, *"Come."* Let Him begin the story of love that starts with your soul being known, healed, and fully embraced. His name is Jesus.

For the one healing after DIVORCE:

You may feel like the chapter has closed, but God is the Redeemer of broken beginnings. He's not just healing your past—He's rebuilding your heart. You do not have to write the next part alone. His arms are stretched wide open, saying, *"Come."* Let Him restore what was lost and rewrite what's ahead.

For the one CARRYING THE MEMORY of a love now gone:

You loved well, and you grieve deeply—and God sees every tear. He holds both your memories and your future. You are not forgotten, and you are not finished. His arms are stretched wide open, saying, *"Come."* Let Him carry you, comfort you, and guide you into the next chapter with grace.

> *"Before you seek a mate, seek the Author.*
> *He writes stories that never fall apart."*

JOURNAL YOUR THOUGHTS

BLESSINGS & REFLECTIONS
Your Heart, His Hands—The Journey Continues

You have now completed this *33-day Introspective Journey of Love and Devotion*. We are grateful, joyful, and in awe of what God is doing. This was not just a book. It was a *journey through prayer*. You planted seeds of trust. You gave God space to speak. You opened your heart to His voice and His timing ... and Heaven took note.

Like He did with Vernestine and me — aligning two hearts 438 miles apart through prayer and divine timing— *He is aligning something beautiful in your life, too*. You are not behind. You are not forgotten. You are not alone. *You are being prepared.*

May your foundation remain firm. May your faith remain fierce. And may you walk boldly into your next season, *hand in hand with God.*

Your Next Step: Take a moment in silence and stillness. Let this question settle in your spirit: *What has God revealed to me, and what will I do with it?* Write it. Pray it. *Declare it with faith.*

Now, lift your hands, lift your heart, and say, "God, I trust You to build my love story on the foundation of prayer. And I am ready for all You have prepared for me."

Blessings & Reflections. Whether you've never been married, are healing from the pain of divorce, or carry the cherished memories of a spouse who has passed, this devotional invites you to pause and reflect—not only on what was lost, but on all that God is still doing. Your story still matters to Him. Every tear, every triumph, every turning point has been seen and held with care. You are not behind—you are being blessed, even now. Take time to reflect on where He has carried you and to recognize the quiet blessings blooming along the way. He hasn't forgotten you, and He's not late. Trust Him. Trust Him. He will not fail YOU. His timing is perfect, and your love story—rooted in grace—is still unfolding, exactly as He designed.

> *"God holds space for your memories and your future; He is not finished with your heart."*

JOURNAL YOUR THOUGHTS

_____
_____
_____
_____
_____
_____
_____
_____

Coming Next in the Invite Him In Series is ...

'Wisdom From the Desk'

Behind every lesson plan is a life lesson.
Behind every classroom door is a calling.

Wisdom from the Desk is a 90-day devotional crafted especially for educators who teach with passion, lead with love, and lean on faith. Whether you're in the classroom, the office, or reflecting after a long day, this devotional invites you to pause, reflect, and hear the voice of the Master Teacher.

Written by a North Carolina Teacher of the Year (1995–1996), this deeply personal journey blends scripture, real-life classroom experiences, prayers, reflections, and affirming quotes that will strengthen your soul and remind you why you were called to teach.

This is more than a devotional—it's a lifeline of hope, wisdom, and faith for educators everywhere.

No matter the challenge, Invite Him In... and watch Him guide your every step—one lesson, one student, one day at a time.

Made in the USA
Middletown, DE
08 August 2025